The Seal
Furry Swimmer

Text by Joëlle Soler
Photos by Fred Bruemmer
Publiphoto/Jacana

Charlesbridge

Copyright © Editions Milan 1990.
300 rue Léon Joulin 31101 Toulouse, France.
Original edition first published by Editions Milan under the title of *le phoque, pêcheur du grand Nord*.

Copyright © 1992 by Charlesbridge Publishing.
Library of Congress Catalog Card Number 92-72904
ISBN: 0-88106-428-9
Published by Charlesbridge Publishing, 85 Main Street, Watertown, MA 02172 • (617) 926-0329
All rights reserved, including the right of reproduction in whole or in part in any form.
Printed in Korea.
10 9 8 7 6 5 4 3 2 1

In the freezing North Atlantic Ocean, where huge sheets of ice crash into each other, harp seals are not cold. Under their fur, they have a thick blanket of fat, called blubber, to keep out the cold and hold in their body heat.

Going south in the winter

Summer is very short up near the Arctic circle where many seals live. Before the cold of winter freezes the ice into solid masses, harp seals begin a long journey south to Canada.

They arrive in the waters near Newfoundland in January, just before the seas there freeze into pack ice. The cold is intense. There is so much ice floating in the water that it looks like ice soup!

In February, the harp seals will have their babies, called pups. First, each mother-to-be carefully chooses a place on the ice. Then she makes a fishing hole through the ice and keeps the hole open and very smooth by going into the water and back out again all day long.

Harp seals are also called saddle seals because the curved black spot on the backs of the older adults looks like a harp or a saddle.

The mother and baby touch noses. The mother knows the unique scent of her own baby.

At birth, the baby's fur is tinted yellow. It weighs about 18 pounds, and its cry sounds a lot like a human baby.

Birth on the ice

At dawn, the wind and the water currents are calm. Many baby seals have been born during the night. The newborn pups are completely helpless. They cannot swim or move very well. Unlike newborn dogs and cats, however, they have their eyes open.

Each pup nuzzles its mother. Like all baby mammals, seal pups drink their mothers' milk. Each mother sniffs her baby and listens to its whimpers so that she will always be able to find her own pup among all the others. Only a few days after her pup is born, she will leave it for a while to go fishing with the rest of the seal herd.

The mother must feed her pup often so that it can build up a layer of fat thick enough to protect it from the cold.

The pup's belly button is pink.

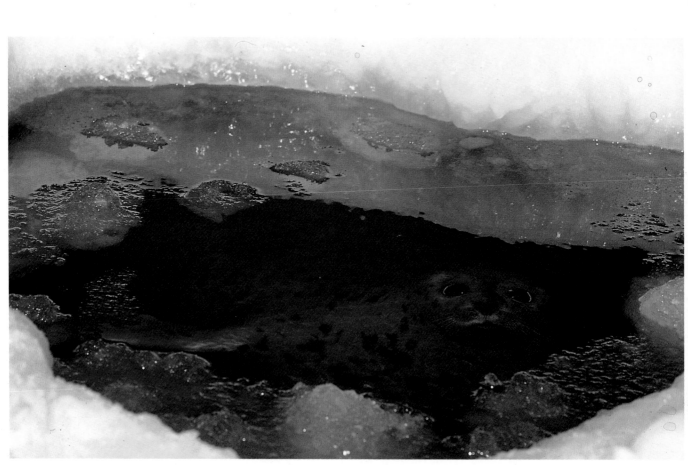

Like all mammals, seals need to breathe air, so they must come to the surface often.

A hungry pup cries out loudly for its mother to feed it.

Another pup makes itself comfortable in the snow and takes its first sunbath.

While the pups wait, the adults fish nearby.

Waiting in a cradle of ice

As the first few days go by, the pup learns to be braver about being left alone. The mother is never away catching fish for very long, but each time, the pup can't wait to be fed and begins to call for her to come back. She pokes her head up through the fishing hole often to check on her little one.

The ice is shaped into choppy hills and valleys by the wind. The pup nestles into the powdery snow. With a belly full of milk, the pup will fall asleep in its cradle of ice.

A loving mother

A curious seal pup goes over to the edge of the hole where it saw its mother disappear, and waits. Suddenly, her glistening grey head rises out of the water. She immediately recognizes her pup by its scent. She jumps out of the water by flapping her powerful rear flippers and gripping the ice with her front claws. Then she rolls over and gives her pup a chance to drink.

The mother feeds her pup five or six times a day. Her milk is ten times richer than cow's milk. Such rich milk helps the pup gain about four pounds a day, and it is soon round and fat.

Is that you, Mom?
Yes, pup. It's time for your lunch.

The mother weighs about 300 pounds and is nearly six feet long. While she is nursing her pup, she will lose two pounds for every one her pup gains.

The mother seal feeds and protects only her own pup.

It is easy to tell which seals are the fathers because they have markings that look like black "hoods" on their heads.

Adapted to life in the water

Harp seals have flippers instead of fins, like fish, or paws, like other mammals. Each front flipper has five webbed fingers with long, sharp claws. The back flippers are very strong so seals can swim fast and can even run across the ice when there is danger.

Harp seals have big eyes and very good eyesight. When the mother dives down into the water to catch fish, she can see in the almost total darkness deep under the ice. When she is on the glaring bright white pack ice, her pupils narrow down to a small slit so that she can still see well.

Sharp front claws can hold on tight to ice and snow.

The shiny white fur lets the sun shine through and warm the pup's skin.

The pup's hind fins will help it make fast turns when it learns to swim.

A harp seal leaves a winding trail when it walks through the freshly fallen snow.

With a keen sense of smell, sharp hearing, and sensitive whiskers, harp seals learn to survive in their icy home.

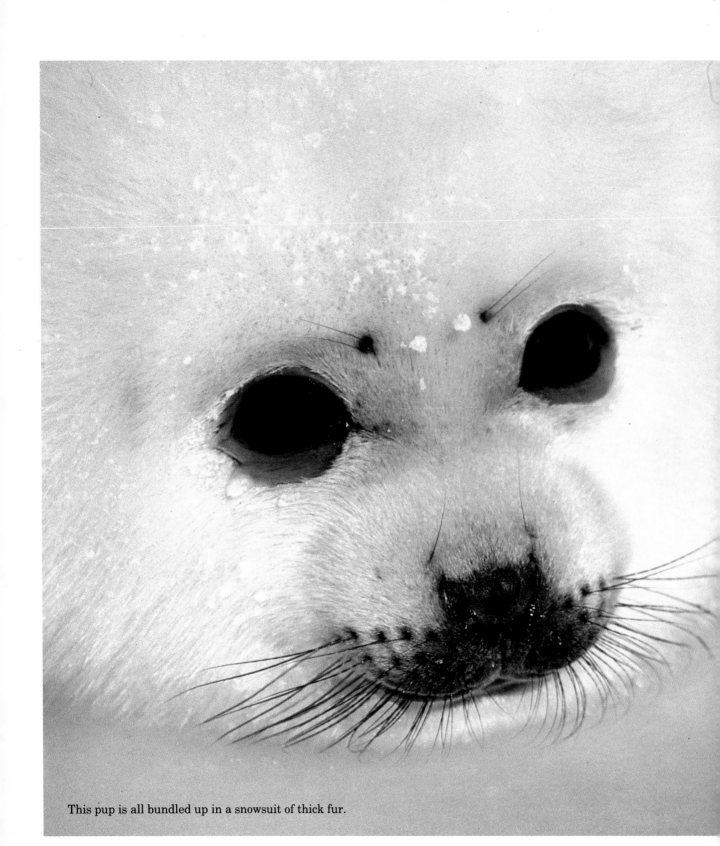

This pup is all bundled up in a snowsuit of thick fur.

The first swim

The mother comforts her wet pup and guides it back to the pack ice.

At ten days old, the plump little pups have grown a lot and do not need to be fed so often. When they are not sleeping or basking in the sun, they like to explore. Even though they are not ready to jump in, the water fascinates them.

A curious pup leans too far over the edge of a hole and kersplash! Its first dive. The water is cold, but the pup now has a thick layer of fat for warmth. The pup floats like a beachball. Its movements are clumsy, and it swallows many mouthfuls of water.

On its first swim, a pup just floats in the water.

Yes, it is true, the young seal does not know how to swim! Luckily, its mother swims quickly to the rescue. She knows that her pup is a little too young to learn to swim.

Using its keen sense of smell, this polar bear can find a seal 18 miles away.

This is the way the female sits up when she senses danger. The only way she can protect herself is by quickly diving through her hole in the ice.

Polar bears do not get along with each other very well and usually fight when they meet.

The danger of the polar bear

Polar bears stay away from places where the pack ice is often broken up by strong sea currents. But where polar bears can easily roam the pack ice, they are a constant threat. Sometimes a hungry polar bear will sit and wait at the edge of a breathing hole until a seal comes up for air.

All of a sudden, a startled mother sits up. She senses danger. With surprising speed, she plunges into the safety of the water. She hopes that her all-white pup will not be noticed by the bear. It is a false alarm. The bear is not interested in food. He is busy looking for a female bear.

A champion diver

By the end of the winter, the mother is very thin. She needs to go fishing to regain her strength. She swims gracefully and can stay under water for more than twenty minutes at a time.

Adult harp seals can dive to a depth of more than 900 feet. They dive to find the little fish they like to eat. Deep under water, it is very dark, but the pupils of a seal's eyes open up very wide. Good eyesight and sensitive whiskers help seals find and catch fish and small shrimp. A seal can eat more than 40 pounds of food a day!

By March, the ice is beginning to melt, and the females have fattened themselves up to prepare for the long trip back to Arctic waters. They will follow the schools of fish that are their food.

The rorqual whale competes with seals for food. They both eat little fish called capelin.

Seals swallow their food while under water, but this seal is spitting out a spin fish that got caught in her throat.

18

This little seal is all alone, waiting for its mother.

When the babies are only a few weeks old, their mothers stop feeding them and rejoin the rest of the herd in the water. The babies must shed their white fur and prepare to join their parents in the water. For about a week, they do not have anything to eat and must live off their own supply of body fat.

Males seldom climb up onto the ice. They wait for the females to join them in the water.

In spring, seals come out of the water for a few days to shed their old fur.

Warning! Danger in the water

By summer time, the seals have shed their old winter fur coats, and they are ready to be on their way back to the Arctic. They will swim about 2,000 miles on their dangerous trip back home. It will take them two to three months to complete this migration.

During their journey, one danger is from killer whales that circle and slowly come to the surface right under the herd of seals. When the killer whales attack, there is panic among the seals. In sprays of foam, the gigantic jaws of the killer whales snap shut. Moments later, the green water becomes calm again. The whales are satisfied with their meal and continue on their way.

Killer whales and sharks are the main predators of harp seals.

21

Once the cute little white pups begin to shed their fur, they begin to look all tattered and raggedy.

Becoming independent

The pups are almost a month old. They are about three times as big as when they were born. They have lost their thick, white fur and have a new waterproof coat. Driven by hunger, they beat their flippers on the ice and finally decide to jump into the water.

They will learn to find fish to eat, and they will begin the long migration to the Arctic. Have a good trip, little furry swimmers!

hen their white fur falls off, the pups will have a new coat
silver fur with black spots.

The end of a massacre

In the last two centuries, the number of seals has been cut in half. The hunters of the world have killed as many as possible to supply fur to people. Today, the massacres are fortunately over. Now the seals see mostly tourists and scientists.

A clothes line with jeans and skins! These skins might have ended up as clothing or boots.

Not very long ago, a hunter could go out on the ice to kill seals.

An unacceptable way of hunting

Less than 50 years ago, people killed harp seals for their fur and for meat. The seal pups were beaten with clubs. It was terrible! Thousands were killed each year. During the 1960's, the public became outraged when films were shown to make people aware of the terrible massacre.

The new tourism
Today, tourists can go to the breeding grounds of the harp seal and visit the pups. Helicopters land on the ice packs, and guides show people how to approach the seals without bothering them.

Scientific research
Scientists are working on several projects to help us learn about this surprising sea mammal.
– Researchers mark pups with colored tags to learn exactly how long they live (about 30 years, they think).
– Scientists study the mysterious survival skills used on the long migration.
– Specialists count seals from an airplane flying over the water to find how many are in each group. They want to know how the seals are competing with people for fish.

A peaceful future?
Today, the harp seal is no longer in danger of extinction. After more than twenty years of international protest, the Canadian government made the hunting of harp seal pups illegal in 1987. Only adult harp seals can be hunted, and only in the open ocean. Now there are about two million harp seals in the North Atlantic Ocean.

Today, one hundred twenty-five thousand seal pups are born every year. They are not afraid of having their pictures taken.

The seal family

There are sixteen members of the seal family. All are carnivorous (fish-eating) marine mammals. Their torpedo-shaped bodies are well adapted to life in the water. They all have ears that are either very tiny or completely inside their heads. They all have nostrils that close when they dive. They all have front paws that have become powerful webbed flippers and are shorter than their back flippers. Seals use only their front flippers to move around on land, unlike sea lions and walruses. When not swimming, seals roll across the ground or slide on the ice. While some seals love to swim in the open ocean, others prefer calm harbors. There are seals all over the world — some in cold waters and others where it is warm.

▲ The Weddell seal is the mammal that lives closest to the South Pole. The female can go without food for five to seven weeks, so she does not have to leave her baby. A Weddell sea can go down as far as 2,000 feet and be under water for as long as forty-five minutes! Amazing

▲ Bearded seals have very thick whiskers. The whiskers help them feel along the sea floor for the shellfish, crabs, and other bottom dwellers they like to eat.

26

Elephant seals are the giants ▶ of the seal family. The males, called pashas, can weigh more than eight thousand pounds and are up to sixteen feet long! When a male gets excited, his nose looks like a short elephant's trunk. Males fight with each other over territory.

Harbor seals are common along the coasts of North America and Europe. They rest on the shore at low tide where they give birth to their young. Harbor seals are very sensitive to pollution.

▲ Monk seals of the Hawaiian Islands are in danger of extinction. During the day, they lie on the golden beaches of small uninhabited islands. At night, they go fishing. Hunted for many years, they are now protected. Let's hope these seals survive!

Photograph credits:
JACANA – Bruemmer/Publiphoto: covers, p 3, p 4-5, p 7 (bottom right), p 8
(top and bottom right), p 9, p 10 (bottom), p 11, p 12 (top right), p 13 (top
right), p 15, p 17 (top), p 18 (bottom), p 19 (bottom and top right), p 22
(bottom right), p 23 (bottom); Danvoye: p 6 (top left), p 14, p 22 (bottom left),
p 25 (bottom); Soler: p 6 (bottom and center), p 7 (top right), p 8 (bottom left),
p 12 (top and bottom), p 13 (top left); Vidal: p 10 (top), p 13 (bottom);
Guravitch: p 16, p 17 (bottom); Gohier: p 18 (top), p 21 (top), p 27;
Varin: p 20-21 (bottom); Ferrero: p 26 (top); Lemoigne: p 26 (bottom).
EXPLORER – Cavaille: p 24 (top); Plisson: p 24 (bottom).
BIOS: p 20 (bottom); Langrand: p 22-23 (bottom).